SEPARATE FLIGHTS

Separate Flights

POEMS

Patricia Hooper

UNIVERSITY OF TAMPA PRESS

Manufactured in the United States of America
Printed on acid-free paper ∞
First Edition

The University of Tampa Press
401 West Kennedy Boulevard
Tampa, FL 33606

ISBN 978-159732-137-2 (hbk.)
ISBN 978-159732-138-9 (pbk.)

Browse & order online at
http://utpress.ut.edu

Library of Congress Cataloging-in-Publication Data

Names: Hooper, Patricia, 1941- author.
Title: Separate flights : poems / Patricia Hooper.
Description: First edition. | Tampa, FL : University of Tampa Press, [2016]
Identifiers: LCCN 2016029484| ISBN 9781597321372 (hardcover : acid-free
　　paper) | ISBN 9781597321389 (softcover : acid-free paper)
Classification: LCC PS3558.O59 A6 2016 | DDC 811/.54--dc23
LC record available at https://urldefense.proofpoint.com/v2/url?u=https-3A__lccn.
loc.gov_2016029484&d=CwIFAg&c=XGugQOAYZ1dlZ6_YqmoVS7m-wN0l
OUpZuda4oPsMe_0&r=8iw8hzd5imWVmmUTCRdyQw&m=3ZHB9uoQ_

for my family

Contents

III. Local Weather

IV. Telling Time

Flying to Nantucket

This is the way my pilot father flew
above the neighborhood, just high enough
so we could see the patterns of the roads,
yet low enough so what we saw was clear.
This morning, off Hyannis, sandy shoals
and cruisers and a ferry flanked by dolphins.
On either shore, a lighthouse, and beyond
each shore, the spire of a church, one dark
with clouds, one lit by sun. We're traveling toward
the sun, six Sunday passengers, a pilot
who barely lifts us up to set us down,
the way my father hovered just above
the trees so we could see the jigsaw fields
that fit between the fences, and our street
that disappeared at last in rows of corn.
I loved the sudden shifts in altitude,
the way he teased us, rising, dropping, dipping
from side to side above the tilting world.
Today Nantucket with its random necklace
of gulls and foam, and years ago the town
seen from a new perspective, not at all
the way it looked close up. I lived to feel it:
the motion of the craft, the way it lifted
into the wind that held it, balancing
above the broad design; the way it turned
to move toward something else, connecting things
I couldn't see without it—steeples, sails
and barns—those bright convergences; the way
it sank to skim the trees, yet took me up.

I

WALKING WITH MERCY

The Heron at Wild Oak Bay

It must have been
a glimpse of the Great Blue Heron
that startled me from abstraction
as it followed me on the road

that morning in Florida.
My mother was sick, and I walked
without seeing, I was so tired,
and all at once it was there
over my left shoulder,
a tall, high-stepping child
or a spindle-legged suitor. It strolled

lightly, as if its feet
were too delicate for the pavement,
and once when I stopped to study
its fog-colored face and an eye
the yellow of swamp water,
it stopped beside me. Oh,

I saw we were comical,
I in my hat and the bird
in black head plumes, our synchronized
striding, but when
we came close to the pond it lifted
and sailed over the house
where my mother slept.

        Grandmother,
who loved her long before I did,
what was it you came to tell me,
dressed in your ghost-grey feathers
from the other world?

Walking with Mercy

Whenever I take the swamp trail through the woods
past the herons in their prehistoric nests,
I keep watch, not for the snakes that slick the path,
but for a sudden stirring, a sharp step
in the understory, and the intense eyes
staring. I can almost believe it's genetic

the way my pulse quickens and my breath shallows
at the possibility I am being scanned,
measured, taken in. Maybe it's my pioneer grandmother
Mercy's startled wariness as she crept
through the forest, hearing Cayuga war cries, the Tory
muskets, her first grandson pressed against her chest;

and how she saw the cabin burning and ran on
into the wilderness, carrying the only one left,
Lebbeus, two years old, who had been berrying
beside her in the thicket when it happened.
Maybe it's she I feel listening through me as I cross
the bridge over the creek bed, close to the rim

where any hand could seize me, though it's only an hour's
walk, not days, nights, almost a week now where she keeps
plodding, barefoot, the child heavy, she can't
go very far, darkness surrounding her—wolves, wildcats,
hunger. She's lost in the Appalachians, trying to find
the settlement she only knows is east, and now I'm at

the fork, the enemy step closer, breath
heavier behind me, only a few minutes to
the parking lot, and she's climbing, she's looking out

over the valley, and when I come to the last bend, she's
lifting the baby, seeing the green farmland, washed clothes
drying on the river bank, the tents and cabins, she's

laughing, she's almost running
into the camp.

Buttons

In Grandma's upstairs closet, the one
with the tall, uncurtained window
that looked down on the yard,
I found a box of buttons: amber glass,
pewter engraved with lilies, shiny black
shoe buttons, and two brass
medallions sporting eagles. There were four,
crystal and faceted, with scraps
of taffeta attached, and one
thin plastic crimson heart.

Maybe those six pearl buttons were the ones
from Grandma's wedding dress. I'd seen
the photograph: she smiled
down at her sleeve, a smile she sometimes gave
to strangers, and her gloved hand
rested on Grandpa's arm.

And that square, enameled pair—
maybe those were the buttons from
the dress she wore to teach
in the one-room school. She walked
four miles through snow, and when
wood for the stove was gone—if one
of the fathers forgot to leave enough—the class
was over. One tall boy
was twenty, older than Grandma was.

I let the buttons trickle through
my fingers, liking the way they chimed
against the metal box—oak toggle bars,
gold roses, ivory shells . . . But when one rolled

under the bottom shelf, too far to reach,
I hurried to put the rest away.

                              Below
the window, in her purple house dress, Grandma
was weeding among the peonies, unaware
that I'd wakened from my nap, or that today
was a day like hundreds of other summer days
that had ended, or that anything was lost.

The Afterlife

I thought that I believed in it but when
my mother was close to death, belief
abandoned me, and she was frightened, she
couldn't imagine not-being, nor could I, it was
unbearable to think of, so I said, "Let's
think about something else, think
about the grandchildren," and I said their names
to calm her, "Jacob, Courtney, Alexandra, Claire,"
and she was quiet, almost seeing them, she said,
"They're precious," and I held her hand, but we
were separate, I was staying in the only world
she wanted—there, on the chair, her slippers, there,
at the window, sun, farther than she could see now, world
where she was *she*, vanishing, and she said again, "I'm
frightened," meaning something language couldn't
speak of, so I said their names again, though she was losing
consciousness, not seeing me, and I was
standing in the room where I'd be standing
after—*Jacob, Courtney, Alexandra, Claire* . . . there was
no other truth to tell her, it was the only
afterlife we had.

Letter to My Mother

November already, and the last brilliant leaves
you saw from the ambulance have dwindled down
to almost none. Summer kept hanging on
all through October, giving us something
to talk about as we stood there at
your graveside feeling stunned,
the way you must have felt, seeing the lamplight
narrow and the voices all
around you on that last night growing dumb.

Today, between bouts of weeping, I've been sorting
through your things. I would have liked the quill
sewing box, but Dad's afraid he'll need
needles and thread to sew his buttons on.
I took your ivory afghan
and the crystal bowl with the gaily scalloped
rim—it must have been Grandma's—
and your antique baby spoons
with the curved handles meant for a child to hold.
And then I couldn't bear to set them out
in their glass-topped curio box when I got home.

One thing I wish I'd asked.
Last spring when you said you wanted me to wear
your diamond ring, I couldn't speak
for grief, although you were talking only
about a distant time. Now I'd like to have the stone
reset as a necklace, and I wonder if
you'd mind. Last night when I tried your ring
it fit perfectly, but you know how I am, always
rummaging in the garden without gloves.
And it seemed strange—whenever I looked down
at my hand, it was your hand holding

a favorite Trollope novel, or smoothing your knitting
pattern, or patting me on my shoulder, gently,
making me turn around.

Small

Small things bring you back. This morning a vague,
tentative snow. Yesterday a blue cup, chipped
when I held it too close to the faucet, ice
crackling, it seemed, until I saw what I had done.
In the garden a few low clumps
of asters I forgot to cut back. Elsewhere, your own
garden's gone to seed, spent flowers
fallen from their stalks, the gardener gone.

It's cold. Not cold enough. Thirty degrees
this morning when I went to feed the birds.
I didn't need my gloves. The storm the local news
predicted all last evening didn't come.
All winter I've been waiting for it: wind
so cold it burns, pond frozen solid, even
the center where the swans were. Heavy snow,
limbs crashing, wires down. The way the air

you gasped for hurt your lungs. I wanted the cup
shattered, cracked clean, a violence to erase what memory
makes of those last days, something you wouldn't want
more of. Instead, a calm
you wanted, a day you wanted. A small breeze
swaying the glass feeder. Small birds come.

By August, Surely

If you spend the whole summer
    weeding, you're bound to see
        not only the busy flowers

but the slippery mold
    sparkling on the lupines,
        the gypsy moth

hovering near the maples,
    the black vine weevil
        with its sticky legs

that can take it up
    the stems of the rhododendrons
        to the faultless leaves, even

the whitefly on the iris,
    which spells ruin. Most of the time
        you forget all about it—spring

with its easy showers, June
    with its chatty branches—
        and then one morning

something is not quite right
    in the garden: a chewed
        blossom, a black stalk. Sometimes

when the mornings are cool
    and lovely, when the asters are crisp
        and lively, I happen to notice

those notches, those sharp
    etchings, and I see
        how others are being carried

into the rich darkness
    beneath them, into the deep
        life of the understory, and I stare

into the face of absence, I try
        to think it—annihilation—I grieve again
            for my mother, who stood among them,

and then,
        unable to change anything,
            I turn back to my basket

of cosmos and beans, I weed
    for a long time in the morning
        of the hummingbird on its errand

and the sun with its perseverance
    and the phlox, the relentless roses,
        and the faithful bees.

Blacksnake

When I noticed the blacksnake I knew
    what had happened to the new rabbits. I didn't
wonder any more about whether they'd find a home

under the pine tree or under the pink magnolia
    where I first saw them, one
still in its nest near the flower pot, one at the door

in Florida, where I came late to a landscape
    of palms and flowers, where I don't know many things—
the pelican, for example, or the armadillo

who dug up my pretty garden, or the Sandhill Crane
    with his pert, red cap on his forehead, his willow legs,
who saw himself in my window and danced and danced,

or the alligator who wandered over the highway
    from the pond to the swimming pool and had to be hoisted
out and carried away. But the newborn rabbits—

no, they were not so lucky. They didn't live
    for forty years like the crane does. They saw only
grass and a few flowers, maybe the sky

and a black vine moving quickly, a dark mouth.
    And now, there he was, the blacksnake, sunning himself,
looking contented, I thought, and a little drowsy

after his morning meal. Well, after all,
    he was here long before I was, so I didn't lift
the shovel and plunge it down on his shimmering body

which has left me its skins, sheer as the skins of onions,
    and kept the mice from my cupboards. I told myself
how he didn't know any different, and off he went

back to the saw palmetto where he disappeared
    to sleep as long as he wanted, hardly disturbing
the path as he swept across it, letting the lawn

close gently behind him, leaving the finches singing,
    the flowers shining, leaving the morning mended
as if nothing had ended, nothing was gone.

II

AT KEATS'S WINDOW

Sunday Flying

Sometimes after the flight show when my father
flew in formation with the other pilots,
diving and somersaulting in his Cessna,
he took us up. The crowd was driving off,
the windsocks disappeared. We flew above
the empty air strip, past the silver hangar,
the ballpark, then the bridge, beyond the school;

and then, if there was fuel enough, we flew
to Hidden Lake where, just below us, Grandpa
was fishing in his rowboat, looking up,
waving his hat, and Grandma hurried out,
wearing her yellow apron. Oh, if only
we could go down and fish for perch with Grandpa!
But it was nearly sunset, and we flew

back over woods and highways toward the town,
and finally there we were above our block,
our house, my Kool-Aid stand, my brother's blue
two-wheeler in the drive. How small it was—
how strange it seemed to look down on your life
from somewhere else. And suddenly I was sick
with loneliness. But we were all together:

my brother with my father up in front,
Mother beside me in the back. And yet
we must be small from *there*: our empty yard,
the Thompsons on their porch, the Barton's airedale
trying to climb the fence, and Mother's clothesline,
my sweater hung to dry. Just then, if I had seen
myself on the swing set, I would not have been surprised.

The View from There

High over Italy
this morning, the sky is filled
with parachutes it seems, but when
they come a little closer—fifty
or sixty of them—every dazzling
undiluted color, sporting stripes,
we see that they've become
hot-air balloons, and dangling
in their baskets, passengers
are waving, heading for
the Alps. They skim

the trees along
the road we're cycling down,
and rise on billowing gusts across
the countryside, then up and
up they go, until it's hard to guess
their altitudes. How leisurely
they seem, drifting above
the hillside towns to reach
those jagged apparitions
tipped with snow.
I'd want to go

too if I hadn't seen
that interview on last night's
local news: how a reporter riding
along a year ago to write the story
of the festival, saw the balloon ahead
lift suddenly and not quite clear
the peaks, then start to sink
toward somewhere just below
the cliffs, and later read
that all aboard
were dead

although from where
he floated, farther still
across the firmament, it looked
like one more graceful if abrupt
descent, and when he leaned to peer
over the rim, he saw what seemed to be
a heap of multi-colored nylon sails
collapsing, or a shining silken tent
pitched on the rocks. Given
that god's-eye-view too far
from earth to hear

the oddly silent
fall, or to observe (before it all
went up in flames) a single fractured
skull, he would have called it beautiful.

At Keats's Window

This must be where you stood
the day you threw your supper
into the street, impatient
and angry in your illness, twenty-five
and dying. Here,
you heard Bernini's fountain,
the broken marble boat,
splashing in the piazza
day and night.

             And here,
your elbows on the sill,
you watched as Doctor Clark
pressed past the flower stalls
and carts of fish to bleed you. You could hear
his footsteps, heavy, pausing
on the stair . . .

When you said you couldn't bear
to open Fanny's letters, Severn promised
to place them in the coffin, on your heart.

Below, in the busy square,
a shopkeeper is shouting
from his shop, and a slender woman
is pushing a baby carriage. It is five
o'clock. On the Spanish Steps
young men loiter and smoke, restless
after work, jostling
to impress the pretty girls.

And no one is looking up
at this narrow room, its niches

already growing dark. A dog runs
freely among the sunny crowds
of tourists, trying to catch
a pair of rolling oranges, barking,
chased by a red-cheeked boy.

Judith

Snow-melt, the freshets rippling through the fields,
and the first green haze furring the sugar maples,
the amelanchiers billowing into flower.
You must be sitting at the window now
in your sun-filled living room, from which you'd see
the waking woods, forsythia, daffodils.
You seemed so calm this morning on the phone,
explaining how the pills no longer work,
no further treatment now, no hope of summer,
and yet no pain, for which the world seems grateful
to overflowing, burgeoning with blossoms.
Six hundred miles away I see you looking
up from your book, the warm sun on your arms,
shading your eyes as if to see more clearly
the near world, and the passage leading through it.

Flare

I was looking out the window at the birds
and maples when it struck me: lightning in
the corner of my eye, fire prickling
in my arms and legs, my scalp
crackling, packed in ice. In the center of
my left eye, summer disappeared, the leaves,
the wall of windows. I fell into
a kitchen chair, too stunned to call
for help, afraid to move. Seconds
later it all came back: the room, my legs and arms
mine again, only a little dizziness, but now
I saw what it could do—before the EEG,
the spinal tap, the MRI—the body turning
inward, against itself. Some god, I thought,
has gripped me, wants me back, but first
it showed me what I was, as if, fallen
into the chair, I somehow swam
above it, staring down, my half-blind eye
compelled to take it in: the plates, the summer day
reflected in the window, everything
I'd thought was mine receding, and the more
I reached for it, the more it fell away.

Two Sojourns in the MRI Machine

1.
Groggy with valium, I've put on the mask
left over from our transatlantic flight.
It kept the movie from my eyes all night,
blocked out the slender cabin rimmed by dusk,
vast darkness, coasts of stars. I must have slept,
if that was sleep, slumped on my daughter's shoulder,
dreaming of moving through a foggy nowhere,
sealed in a crowded capsule, funneled between
black ocean, emptiness. And then we dropped
a little, till I looked. Still black, still lost.
Only the stars swam in their silver mirror,
the moon still crossing what we must have crossed.
And then, toward dawn, a steel-blue glaze, a slash
of crimson, England beneath us, green and lush,
familiar as my child, my shoes, my sweater.
Descent, the force of land, the news of weather,
the reassuring captain's welcoming voice,
a breeze through the opening tunnel. It was over.

2.
In Rome, at the catacombs,
I took three steps inside the corridor,
drew one dank breath, and fled. All that I saw
were the first vaults where Christians kept their bones
although their souls, as they believed, had risen.
Outside, I sipped gelato melted down
in a plastic bowl and waited for my daughter
who moved inside the earth. All that the gods
would have to do was roll one boulder over
the entrance . . . But the guard looked bored, our driver,

who'd seen so many leave the underworld,
sprawled on a blanket near the parking lot
and smoked, and up the hill, a plot of asters,
a path, a shop, a fountain spilling water,
and then, around the curve, thank god, my daughter.

The Missing Pilot

Whenever we picked my father up from work
we visited the hangar where the Seabees,
Cessnas and Piper Cubs were lined in rows,
and Tom and Bob were working on the engines,
ready to stop and lift us to the cockpits.
Our friends had pets, but what we had were airplanes
like horses people stabled somewhere else.
Today mine was the Cessna: I was Lindbergh
crossing the ocean, then Amelia Earhart
solo above Hawaii, and my brother
was dropping bombs on Tokyo and Berlin.
At night our paper airplanes did chandelles,

littering chairs and tables. Then the phone rang,
a silence in the kitchen. Father grabbed
his coat and said a Piper Cub was lost
over Lake Huron—nothing on the radar—
he'd have to join the search. All night in bed
I flew alone and dreamed of where he was,
black winter sky, no lights for miles, the moon
scanning the icy water, and no sign
of anything except the lake for hours.
At dawn my mother stood beside the window,
watching the road, then flicked the radio
to news, but there was nothing, only weather:
more freezing rain, more snow. She started sweeping,

then dusting, sorting through the kitchen drawers,
then cookies in the mixer, in the oven.
She turned the pages of the morning paper,
watered the plants, and stared. I seemed to be
drawing a house and trees, but I was sinking

through deepening water to the sandy floor.
Above, a searchlight, moving past me. *Someone
could disappear . . . and yet he must be somewhere,
and I was . . .* Why could Mother hardly see me
when I was in the room? I watched her frown,
mend stockings, watch the road until, at lunch time,
she made us soup and crackers, read a story,
and everything was as it was before.
Except for when she sighed . . . and oh, the look
on Father's face that night when he returned,
as if he hardly knew us, through the door.

Red Sled

An ice storm's glassed
the garden, brittle trees
ticking in wind, and while

I'm looking, a branch snaps
from the sugar maple, spirals
down to the snow bank where

you rode your new red sled
moments before. A chill—
a thin shard—passes through me.

Up! Up! I lift you up
to the window: there's the tree,
the long gash near the top,

and down below, the sled
deep in the drift, half-buried
by the severed limb, yet somehow,

thanks to the snow, intact.
Or so it seems—it's still
too risky to venture out

though you want your jacket zipped
and wave one mitten, *Go!*
No, let's take off our coats,

and after the ice melts
and the breeze dies down, I'll lift
the branch, or someone will—

I'll need help—but for now
you're sitting in my lap
watching your mittens drip,

the usual miracle.

The Radio Flyer

1.

The poster paints and easel
I'd seen uptown and asked for
were under the Christmas tree,
but the crimson metal wagon
with words along each gleaming
side, and the black handle,
was something I'd never seen.
My mother read the words
aloud, *Radio Flyer*,
and even before I noticed
the gift tag dangling
from the green bow on the handle,
my brother read his name.

2.

I was drawing circles in the small
puddle beneath the eaves, the one that filled
with birthstones when it rained. On other days
the stones were dull as sand. No one but I
knew they were there: emerald and amethyst,
ruby and sapphire—colors
of the rings in Woolworth's window
just last week. When I looked up,
pleased with my secret, something caught
my eye: the Radio Flyer
vanishing down the block, my brother riding
with a friend, pulled by another friend.

3.

I filled it with the baby blankets Mother
let me use, and then my dolls—Peggy
and Carol Ann and Betsy and Georgina
whose name was on her dress. I put
my tea set in Georgina's lap and pulled
the wagon down the driveway
toward the tree. It was so hot—I thought
of running through the sprinkler,
but I could use the wagon
for the day . . .
          I held
the dolls up slowly, letting each one stand
to see how glad the others were to sit
in the wagon, looking out, and then I fed them
and put them back and pulled them
to the corner. Not one of them had to wait
for her turn, under the tree.

4.

Father wore his flight jacket, brown leather
with fur inside the collar, and my brother
sat in the student pilot's seat. We flew
over the fairgrounds while my brother tried
the instruments, though whenever the plane dipped
or rose abruptly, just to make us gasp,
I knew that it was Father in control.
I sat beside my mother, wanting nothing
but to be taken up above the fields,
the roads, the dizzying trees. I closed my eyes
and I *was* flying, nothing holding me
except my outstretched arms, the way I flew

at bedtime down the stairs, across the garden,
over the swing set, high above our house
and out across the bay . . . then back again:
familiar streets below, the empty yard,
our sleeping house, the moonlit car, the wagon.

5.

At the end of summer Mother let us walk
two blocks to Webber's store. I stayed outside
with the wagon while my brother went to buy
milk and a loaf of bread. I longed to see
the glass case with the gum drops, sourballs,
and licorice, and choose my own, but what I wanted
most was to guard the wagon. When a girl
came out with a bar of soap, she said she wanted
a wagon just like mine. I didn't say
that it was mine. Or wasn't.

6.

Mother took us to the park to gather
chestnuts, helping us pull the wagon
along the gravel path. The grass was heaped
with chestnuts, some in their green husks,
the others dark, revealed. One had a stem
and leaf attached, and Mother let me keep it
for kindergarten while we tossed the others
into the wagon, hundreds to hide for treasures
or roll downhill or use for paperweights
or checkers or paint with faces—Mother had
an endless list of possibilities. . . .
We pulled the wagon home, each of us taking
turns, and neither seemed to care

who pulled, who rode. One side was dented in,
one wheel wobbled. When I put my share
of the chestnuts in a bag, I left the wagon
waiting beside the porch, and a month later,
when I walked home from school in the first snowfall,
it was still sitting there.

III

LOCAL WEATHER

Goldfinch

Something
flashed through the world this morning,
a spangle, a spark.

It skittered across the lilacs
and flared in the junipers, then
ricocheted off the maple—

a candle, a coin, a comet.
Then it spun through the crab apple
and zigzagged across the begonias

and sailed out over the rims
of the lindens, taking the sun
with it behind the clouds.

Now the rain falls as expected.
Now I stand on the back porch
or sit by the window, I hardly

dare to glance down for an instant, for now
who knows what will happen, what
will appear, what I will see

the next time that glittering notion
flits through the heart.

Monet Paints the Willows, 1918

He had just set down his brush
and closed his eyes—they seemed
much cloudier today—to see
the blue-washed leaves more clearly
in his mind. And then he heard,
or thought he heard, the sound
of distant thunder.

        No,
no, he thought, no need
to put away his paints
and move inside. It was
a burst of cannon fire in the Somme.

On the table near his chair
the maid had placed a slice
of cake and jam—so pretty
when he looked at it again, although
a vulgar fly had landed
on the tray.

        Just yesterday
he'd spurned the chance to leave
or send his paintings off
to safety. No, if the Germans came,
they'd find him in his studio among
his water lily canvases: he'd die
in the midst of what he'd done.

He dozed, and when he woke
the air was quiet—only
an intermittent breeze
and faint artillery fire from Amiens.

And since his rested eyes
no longer blurred, he'd work
a little longer in the balmy air.

                              It was
an almost-perfect day, late morning sun
high in the willow leaves, the pond
shimmering, undisturbed . . .

In the Gallery

Another Dutch landscape—
    this one a low plain, sea water
        seeping through the grass.

And the flat sky behind it—indigo—but first
    the mahogany-red farmhouse,
        the windmill's wings turning

through mist in the gold light.
    Didn't you tell me
        you cut across wet fields

on the way to your grandmother's?
    There's the tidy path, there's the gnarled
        wind-hammered tree

and the place someone has walked
    over bent weeds. Oh, why do I
        add you to everything,

even here? Isn't what's left enough?

No Clearing

I left the windows open when
I locked my house. Rain
began as I drove away.

Too late to turn back now. I rushed
to the hospital where my friend
lay comatose, the cancer
accruing in her brain. Last night
she barely seemed to breathe.

But now the tubes were gone,
and when I spoke, a smile
floated across her face.
She seemed to notice me.

"It's just a reflex," offered
the cheerful nurse who'd come
to read the vital signs.
"She's almost gone—it's good
you came today."

Back home the rain had poured
over the sills. I barely
saw as I mopped it up,
and now, at evening, rain

and clouds are thicker still
as forecast, not a scrap
of sky. It startles me
that I should feel relieved
to see how, for a moment,
things look like what they are.

The Guest

After she left I went back into the house. The plants needed watering. I had forgotten about them for a long time.

Upstairs I noticed the bed carefully made and the chair moved out from the wall where she must have put on her shoes. The curtain was turned back where she'd opened and closed a window in the night.

I could hear the furnace starting up for a moment, but it stopped. In the study my desk was waiting, and the books I'd been reading a week ago were still hidden away in the shelves. I took down *Mrs. Dalloway* and *Conifers for Small Spaces*.

I could open a desk drawer or pick up a magazine or go out to fill up the feeder. I went into the hall and came back. Sometimes I leafed through the soft, leather-bound notebooks I'd bought in Murano. At noon, when the phone rang, I was still trying to choose between intimate pleasures.

Downpour

A sudden, intense rain spills
over the beach towels
I've hung to dry, then stops
as abruptly as it came. The July sky,
like a calm face after anger,
holds only a single cloud.

Now hours will pass before
the sodden wash swings light
and free again, and the daylilies
that sag over the fence
lift up their heavy flowers.

Such a lot of trouble
from a fleeting thing!
And what I said to you—
how many days
or weeks will pass before
it no longer weighs you down?

Mid-August:

                              the sun barely
up over the maples, squirrels

busy beneath the feeder, even
the grass rampant again

after weeks of heat. Out here
by the woodpile, the sun ripples

like water, a chill steam
rising, although by noon

we won't notice: eighties again, the car
warm when I drive to town. Only

this slippage, mornings, late
sunrise, the birds quieting. I keep

going out and in, restless, inventing
errands—a weed, a melon—the lawn

darker, long shadows in
the beans, under the vines.

First Day

The melons swell and tumble near the fence,
and summer squash still ripen though the school bus
delivers neighbor children back to school.
Their yards are empty like the ones I passed
on Maple when I used to walk the block
to North School in my new fall shoes and dress.
How quickly summer vanished! Coming home
it was time, almost, for supper and for bed.

                         Last night the radio
warned of a chance of frost. These green tomatoes
should be taken in today to ripen under
newspapers, and a last cool-weather crop
of spinach should be sown. But it's too hot—
nothing has changed, not visibly, and yet
the cardinal's song, which always seemed so cheerful,
seems hesitant, equivocal, and vast.

In Autumn

Clouds go over. The maples flare again.
In the garden the last bright asters
blaze in the autumn air
the way my skin burned
when you turned to me
in the chill breeze off the lake.

The days are cool now,
the nights are deep, and long.
At the feeder a red-winged blackbird
has come in from the fields
and sorts among the seeds.
A rare visitor—
even if he finds what he wants
he'll never stay here.

These are the last days.
Already the stalks of lilies
have withered, and the gold petals
of the rose melt on the grass.
But the sky flames, more intense.
I didn't see it coming.
For the few days you were here with me
all the familiar warnings disappeared.

Mulching Season

When the last ornaments lie
in their tissue paper nests
I bring in the hedge pruners.
No more dragging the tree whole
from the front door to the curb.
I dismantle it branch by branch
while it stands in my living room window.

Out in the garden a faint
snow is already falling,
but I know where the phlox sleeps
under its thin blanket,
and the fussy delphinium and
a few favorite lilies.
I choose ruthlessly, then
scatter the stiff boughs.

Back in the house, the trunk
stands in its red planter,
plucked clean, ready to burn.
Oh, all the immense plans—
the wrappings and unwrappings!
the trimmings and untrimmings!
Before I carry it out
to the woodpile, the mail arrives
with a late Christmas card and the spring
seed catalogue from Burpee.

The Cardinal

I was writing about the cardinal when it landed on the telephone wire just outside my window. Which to watch—the image or the bird?

And I don't know which gave me the most pleasure, the silk flourish of cardinal who, after a few moments, sailed off into the arborvitae, or the smooth strokes of my pen flying across the page, free of effort for the first time all fall.

Keep going, the cardinal said, then, *Watch me, watch me*. If I wasn't careful, the whole Saturday morning would be lost.

Isn't this a strange habit, writing about life while still living it? If only one could be assured of clear memory and enough puzzlement and a pen and paper later on.

Blue Heron

Every morning
the heron took
one long, measured step
after another.

That's how I saw it
in Sarasota:
from the shallow pool
to the shining inlet

could take a long time.
You could lift one foot—
you could stand so still
not a fish could hear you—

you could lift the other.

Meanwhile, the minnows
swam busily back and forth.

*

Sometimes I sit
with the white paper
and I write one word,
then
        another.

A long time passes.

Something glitters
near the silky surface
of the mind's waters,

something fleeting and
possibly delicious.

When I see it
I move fast.

*

All winter the heron
waded among the minnows
and the tasty crabs
and the murky catfish,

each one bustling
with its own excitements,

so they hardly noticed
the grey pillar
that stood above them.

Then its head tilted.

Then its beak dipped
down.

*

It may be enough
to dart through the world freely
in its flashing waters,

or to soar above it
on its milky currents,

but what I saw
is how every morning
the heron waited

and stepped slowly
and reached quickly

and caught something
so satisfying

it stretched upward
in its awkward body

and grew lighter
and sailed away.

IV

TELLING TIME

At the Equinox

Three days in the eighties, then
a chill morning, the beech tree
beginning its gold descent.

And the red domes of the maples
through which we saw
the rimmed sun as it weakened,

the geese rallying.
Already the pine siskin,
itinerant visitor

at the strewn deck of the feeder,
the hawk still circling.
And the crimson asters, the garden

too earnest, sustained brilliance
an effort we recognized.
That day we gathered

late peaches, the year's first apple
with its dense, interior snow—
the end and the beginning—

while the sun passed
over the planet's center.
We felt it, didn't we,

as if we were one body,
an approaching darkness
equivalent now to the light.

How Far

My mother-in-law calls to tell me that it's dark.
"I thought you ought to know," she says, her voice
solicitous in her house an hour away.

The best day she had all week
was the day I took her shopping, and *I* got lost.
"They must have changed the streets around," she said.
"Where are you taking me anyway, Pennsylvania?"

But sometimes she calls to ask me where she is.
"I must be in a hospital except
my furniture is here. This can't be right.
I'm frightened—is this someone else's house?"

It *is* dark when she calls
tonight, and darker still when I look out
at the deep, blackening sky where even the moon
is missing, and my living room, well-lit,
shines out on nothing visible. My book,
my chair . . .

                Last week she called to ask,
"How far is this? Will I be here tomorrow?"

A Long Marriage

All afternoon the weather changed, then deepened
as if there might be snow, but it was something
she hadn't seen before at the kitchen window,
and he, reading the *Times* or pruning dahlias,
felt he should be getting ready, but for what
he couldn't have said. At supper they both started
to ask if the other noticed: a changed sky,
falling barometer, or something else
that made the month seem earlier. Or later.
But they were shy, as they seldom were, together,
and when they looked outside it was July
along the street, and others were still mowing
or weeding. It was something in her mind,
presentiment, she thought, and when they listened
to the evening news, he saw that what he'd sensed
was not reportable, it was his own.
And then she spoke. He spoke. And what bewildered
each was not that it was here, this feeling
of something coming closer—something they wouldn't
have named now if they could, for they recognized it
for what it was, a dread, interior weather—
but that it had come to both of them at once.

A Box of Trout Flies

Look what your father left you,
these caddis flies tied by his hands

and tucked in their tiny compartments—
Brown Sedges of seal fur or rabbit

fastened with cinnamon silk,
and these Dark Blue Sedges, grey mallard

with ribs of gold wire, so sprightly
they seemed to have hatched from the stream

and flown straight to your doorstep. And here
are their cousins, the mayflies—Quill Gordons

with torsos of peacock, March Browns
sporting fox fur and pheasant. And look

at these Coffin Flies, Leadwing Coachmen
with their forelegs held out to shake hands.

All winter, the river snowbound,
he sat by the fire and fashioned

these dry-flies—spinners and duns—
and dreamed of the caddis hatching

in April on the Au Sable,
and later in summer, the mayflies

pocking the stream where the trout
lie hidden and cunning. And now,

if you look, you can see him again
after so many years, wading out

to the rock where the water is colder
and the clever ones no one can catch

lie close to the bottom. The caddis
are dropping, the fish are rising,

and there is your father, his creel
ready, his eye on the rock

where the current has pooled. He is matching
his bait to the hatch, he is casting

his line over the rapids
and setting alight on the surface

a fly so alive, so convincing
even the flies are fooled.

Inscriptions

There they are, just as expected,
three lines etched in my forehead—
three years of piano lessons—

and that long, vertical fault
from Algebra II. "Stop scowling,
stop squinting," my mother warned,

years ago. "You'll have crow's feet
around your eyes." I confess
to those fine furrows, the tracks

birds leave over snow, their impressions
like faint thoughts, growing deeper.
Today, passing the mirror,

I wondered what grim morning
of frowning imbedded its stamp
at the bridge of my nose, what sorrow

eroded my cheek to remain
years after it should have passed.
And those curves engraved at the corners

of my surprised mouth . . .
When you kissed me suddenly once
and again, and for years after,

was it you who set out to blur
the print of this curious text,
these signatures, so that today

when I studied them in the mirror,
I couldn't be perfectly sure
which was pain, which was pleasure.

Clear Morning

Today the rain has ended, and the sun
returns as it always does
after an absence: dominant,
more intense.

Everything comes back:
the hummingbird finding its way
to the throat of the morning glory, bees
ravishing the flowers.

I pace among the wet trees, not knowing
what to do with so much longing—
nothing prepared me for it,

not the rain or the leaves,
not even the garden with its bright petals
spilling on the grass.

When you were leaving
I trusted those distractions, turning
quickly to the faithful
that could save me,

but they were powerless
as angels, never having known
the coursing of the soul
within the body.

They shone.   They fled.

At the Terminal

Remember how we took those separate flights
imagining the worst: our plane gone down,
our children young, alone? I'd leave an hour
before you, wait to meet you at your gate,
or you'd go first, arrive and rent a car,
then meet me at the exit. In between,
blue emptiness, our lives suspended where
clouds stacked themselves between us: you on earth
and I already gone. Or else I'd stand
on solid ground and watch you disappear—
my heart, my shining bird!—a streak of light,
a flash of wing, then nothing. Only one
of us, one at a time. And whether I turned
back to the concourse or pulled down the shade
over the brilliant window, belted in
above the tilting tarmac, I rehearsed
this hour, ever nearer, when the planet
would hold one or the other, and you'd watch—
or I—the earth receding, or look up
into the arc of absence, blinding space.

Blue Window

1.
On the morning my granddaughter
appeared in the world I was washing
windows, broad sweeps of sky
clearing, a plane passing
under my paper towel
and disappearing, dissolved
in the pink clouds of the dogwood.
It might have been
my father flying his Cessna
into the present, tipping
his wing as he went over,
and so when the phone rang
with the news, it was hard to tell
where the room ended and sky
began as I stood talking, only
a thin lens between me
and the plane, this world
and the next one.

2.
And on the day
my grandmother died I was peeling
oranges. I wish I could say
I noticed the light changing,
some slippage, but everything stayed
as it was: table and chairs,
the blue vase full of flowers.
I must have been making
breakfast and stood watching
a cardinal at the feeder,
while what she was seeing—

sun on her porch, leaves
blowing, the usual bees
in the bells of the hollyhocks—
stopped.

3.
And on the day
my mother died, a day
I am never far from, I stood
holding her hand and the nurse
said she was gone already
although she was breathing, her body
unable to wind down
from so many years of living,
and in the room
her sweater was waiting, a bead
of water slid down the glass
tumbler beside her, and I
was still in the world when it spilled
to the nightstand, and she
was not.

4.
And someday
when my granddaughter is learning
the alphabet or deciding
which college which boy or driving
her daughter to school, I will slip
through a surface as clear as the storm door
I'm washing this morning, the one
on which a mosquito has landed,
trying to get—tell me—
in? out?

Fall Sequence

On the last morning of summer
my garden revives, flaunting
its golds, crimsons, and yellows—
one dance before disappearing.
My ninety-year-old father
frolics about the house.

*

A damp chill near the woodpile.
Now only the cedar waxwings
stop by the feeder, excited
acquaintances here for a morning,
breakfasting, hurrying south.

*

Mice move to the cellar, spill
seeds in the storeroom, die
in the mouse traps. I toss them
into the pine grove. Nothing
stirs on the forest floor.

*

Leaves fall to the porch, litter
the lawn under the maples.
Raking this morning I find
my grandmother's locket, buried
for years under the moss.

*

The leaf pile goes up
in smoke, sending
its sparks into the branches.
For a few seconds they float there
under the other stars.

*

Early November. Now
when I look at the garden I see
only the snow falling
miles north, on my mother's grave.

The Seabee

In June when Mother drove us to the lake
my father stayed behind, but Friday mornings
he flew up in his Seabee, circling over
the cottage till we ran outside and waved.
He tipped one sunlit, silver wing, then landed
and taxied to the dock. Even before
he stepped down from the cockpit, neighbor children
came running to greet him: clearly, this was fame.

At night, when the woods and lake grew dark, I slept
on the screened-in porch where I could watch the Seabee
rocking and the moon stroking its wings.
One morning waves rolled in—the beach was gone—
and when my brother and I ran out to swim,
racing to reach the plane, a buoyant spill
of iridescent fuel slipped past our arms;

and then too high a wave, and I was swept
under the dock where water struck the boards
and sand from the bottom roiled so thick I knew
that only the power that sent me plunging under
could pull me back. For a long moment while
I caught my breath, unnerved, I didn't panic
but watched from churning water how the sun
shone through the slats as if the day went on

without me, as before. And then I saw
how it would be: the cots and chairs put back
in storage, car doors closing, and the Seabee
waiting, its silver undersides, the first
familiar, sputtering, finally deafening sound
of its propeller, gaining, and its wake
above me, as it steadied, lifting off.

At the Rifle River

When the eagle unfurled, clearing
the green dome of the forest,
I almost missed it

till somebody cried, "Look up!"

and there it was
in the sky over the river

which I saw it must have owned
the way it spanned the rapids
with a single stroke,

and the sky parted.

I can't say I believe
in messengers from the clouds,

but I didn't believe
this was an accident either,

the way its light
tore through the drab morning
I barely lived in, and then

it rose over the steaming
forest, it disappeared.

*

At the time I was only watching
my own path by the river,

but afterward
I knew it must still be there
over the rim of maples,

its white helmet, its fire,
and its gold eye turned toward me,

or something enough like it,
something powerful and amazing
which someone else sees.

Imagine my certainty
the moment before it rose
through the world, crossing the water,
that there was nothing anymore to surprise me.

Imagine my emptiness.

Imagine my surprise.

Telling Time

The night when the moon silvered
the sky at ten below zero,
and Orion shone in the heavens,
and the ponds froze into iron,

the Great Horned Owl came down
out of the clouds, carving
her way through the channels of cold
to the heronry on the island.

Then she called in the dawn, then she mated
in the faint snow, flying inland,
and sailed back alone to the heron's
basket, forty feet up. In the season

of sleeping turtles, the fox's
hunger, the Great Horned Owl
returned to her task, and if now
she remembered the rabbit's cry

or the cracked bones of the squirrel
in the sun, there was no sign
but herself as the wind drove hard
through the heron-bare trees, its message

a wolf's howl as she waited
high and alone. And in time,
on the morning the ponds thawed
all at once, and the snowdrops

pushed up from the netherworld,
and the frogs woke, and the willows
furred, and the red-winged blackbirds
swept in from the south, still steaming,

the Great Blue Herons came riding,
ripping the sky with their sticks,
weaving the trees, repairing
their penthouse of ragged platforms

except for one where the owl
watched over her own. And tonight,
on an evening when spring peepers
sing from the swamps, and the mud

ripples with salamanders,
and tree swallows are sweeping
the caddis-strewn streams, the owl
unfolds from her nest and sails down

to the tamaracks, coaxing her young
to the reeds, to the frog-brimming ponds
and the skittering grasses, waking
the turtle, the crow, till the marsh

reappears, teeming and wild,
as she lifts, as she rides out
on the currents of spring—as she calls them
into the world.

Acknowledgments

Grateful acknowledgment is made to the editors of the following publications in which some of these poems first appeared:

AGNI: "A Long Marriage," "Blacksnake"

Alaska Quarterly Review: "Monet Paints the Willows, 1918"

The American Scholar: "In the Gallery"

Arts & Letters: "Blue Heron," "Clear Morning," "No Clearing"

The Atlanta Review: "Walking with Mercy"

Cave Wall: "At the Rifle River"

Cold Mountain Review: "Goldfinch"

The Hudson Review: "The Afterlife," "At the Terminal," "By August, Surely," "Buttons," "Fall Sequence," "In Autumn" (as "Equinox,") "Judith," "Letter to my Mother," "The Heron at Wild Oak Bay"

The Iowa Review: "The Seabee," "Two Sojourns in the MRI Machine"

Michigan Quarterly Review: "Telling Time," "The View from There"

Mid-West Quarterly: "First Day, "Mid-August"

Nimrod: "The Missing Pilot"

Orion: "Small"

Poet Lore: "How Far"

Shenandoah: "At the Equinox"

Snowy Egret: "Mulching Season"

Southern Humanities Review: " Flying to Nantucket,"

   "Inscriptions"

The Southern Review: "A Box of Trout Flies," "At Keats's

   Window," "Blue Window," "Downpour," "Flare"

Several poems also appeared in anthologies: "At the Terminal" in *On the Wing*, edited by Karen Yelena Olsen, University of Iowa Press, 2005; "In Autumn" (as "Equinox") in *The Heart of Autumn*, edited by Robert Atwan, Beacon Press, 2001; "A Box of Trout Flies," "The Heron at Wild Oak Bay," and "The Seabee" in *The Southern Poetry Anthology: North Carolina*, Volume VII, edited by William Wright, Texas University Press, 2014; "Blacksnake" in the online anthology, *Poetry Daily*. "The View from There" was awarded the 2011 Laurence Goldstein Award for Poetry from *Michigan Quarterly Review*.

Special thanks to Suzanne Stryk for providing her painting, "Blue Vortex #2," for the cover.

*

"At the Rifle River" is dedicated to Carolyn Owen and to the memory of Thomas E. Owen; "Judith" to the memory of Judith Goren; and "Telling Time" to Daniel Minock, who took me to see the owl he wrote about in his book of essays, *Thistle Journal* (Mid-List Press, 1998).

About the Author

Patricia Hooper is the author of three previous books of poetry: *Other Lives*, *At the Corner of the Eye*, and *Aristotle's Garden*. She is also the author of a chapbook, *The Flowering Trees*, and four children's books. Her poems have appeared in many magazines, including *The Atlantic Monthly*, *The American Scholar*, *Poetry*, *The Hudson Review*, *Ploughshares*, *The Southern Review*, and *The Kenyon Review*. A graduate of the University of Michigan, where she earned B.A. and M.A. degrees, she has been the recipient of The Norma Farber First Book Award of the Poetry Society of America, The Bluestem Award for Poetry, a Writer's Community Residency Award from the National Writer's Voice, and the Laurence Goldstein Award for Poetry from *Michigan Quarterly Review*. She lives in North Carolina.

About the Book

Separate Flights has been set in Janson Text, a digital font based on matrices originally cut by the Hungarian-Transylvanian priest Miklos Kis (1650-1702) and named in honor of the Dutch printer-publisher Anton Janson, who used the types during the seventeeth century and was believed for many years to have created them. The original matrices survived in the holdings of the Stempel Foundry in Germany, and they were highly valued by D. B. Updike, Stanley Morison, and others concerned with the revival of fine printing. The book was designed and typeset by Richard Mathews at the University of Tampa Press.

Poetry from the University of Tampa Press

John R. Bensko, *Visitations*◊

John Blair, *The Occasions of Paradise**

Michelle Boisseau, *Among the Gorgons**

Bruce Bond, *Black Anthem**

Jenny Browne, *At Once*

Jenny Browne, *The Second Reason*

Jenny Browne, *Dear Stranger*

Christopher Buckley, *Rolling the Bones**

Christopher Buckley, *White Shirt*

Richard Chess, *Chair in the Desert*

Richard Chess, *Tekiah*

Richard Chess, *Third Temple*

Kevin Jeffery Clarke, *The Movie of Us*

Jane Ellen Glasser, *Light Persists**

Benjamin S. Grossberg, *Sweet Core Orchard**

Benjamin S. Grossberg, *Space Traveler*

Michael Hettich, *Systems of Vanishing**

Dennis Hinrichsen, *Rip-tooth**

Patricia Hooper, *Separate Flights*◊

Kathleen Jesme, *Fire Eater*

Jennifer Key, *The Old Dominion**

Steve Kowit, *The First Noble Truth**

Steve Kowit, *Cherish*

Lance Larsen, *Backyard Alchemy*

Lance Larsen, *Genius Loci*

Lance Larsen, *In All Their Animal Brilliance**

Julia B. Levine, *Ask**

Julia B. Levine, *Ditch-tender*

Sarah Maclay, *Whore**

Sarah Maclay, *The White Bride*

Sarah Maclay, *Music for the Black Room*

Peter Meinke, *Lines from Neuchâtel*

John Willis Menard, *Lays in Summer Lands*

Kent Shaw, *Calenture**

Barry Silesky, *This Disease*

Jordan Smith, *For Appearances**

Jordan Smith, *The Names of Things Are Leaving*

Jordan Smith, *The Light in the Film*

Lisa M. Steinman, *Carslaw's Sequences*

Lisa M. Steinman, *Absence & Presence*

Marjorie Stelmach, *Bent upon Light*

Marjorie Stelmach, *A History of Disappearance*

Ira Sukrungruang, *In Thailand It Is Night*◊

Richard Terrill, *Coming Late to Rachmaninoff*

Richard Terrill, *Almost Dark*

Matt Yurdana, *Public Gestures*

* Denotes winner of the Tampa Review Prize for Poetry
◊ Denotes winner of the Anita Claire Scharf Award